This invaluable workbook belongs to:

STRENGTHS EXPLORATION WORKBOOK

Team Edition

Strength 1:

Strength 2:

Strength 3:

Strength 4:

Strength 5:

STRENGTHS EXPLORATION WORKBOOK
Team Edition

What to do After you get your List of Strengths

© 2017 All Rights Reserved, including the right of reproduction in whole or in part in any form.
ISBN: 978-1541367593
Published by Focal Star Publishing, California, USA

Table of Contents

Introduction   1

My Strengths Reference   5

Strengths Review   9

Strength Domains   13

Individual Strengths   17

Understanding Your Team's Strengths   37

Team Grid   47

Optimum vs. Overused   53

Trigger Strength   57

% I Work in My Strengths   61

Strength Tracking   67

Job Responsibilities   85

Continuing the Change   89

Quick Reference   93

Success is achieved by developing our strengths, not by eliminating our weaknesses.

- Marilyn vos Savant

INTRODUCTION

There are many resources to help you minimize your weaknesses, however, research shows that you can get a greater return from the same investment when you focus on improving your Strengths.

The focus of this workbook is to help you and your team to understand your Strengths, identify how they work in your life already, and create a plan to maximize those Strengths.

Our first instinct whenever we are graded, evaluated or assessed is to quickly scan through what you did well and to find where you messed up. Everyone wants to know where their biggest faults are so that they can pour more time and attention into fixing themselves.

One of the reasons for the success of Strength Based training is that at its foundation is the truth that we all possess valuable qualities. There is potential inside everyone and when we connect that talent with skills, knowledge and purpose you've got a Strength that breathes life into that person and those around them.

The key is to move past the concept that the only way to improve is to fix our faults. We need to take ownership of our future by actively engaging in a process to become more of who we are destined to be. There is a rich potential just waiting to be discovered. You've started the process aleady by coming to this workshop. Are you ready to move through the exercises and do the extra work it entails? Or will you simply sit back and wait for this "Strengths" fad to pass, all the while knowing that others are coming alive through this process?

The research into understanding your Strengths has set a foundation upon which millions have come to understand they were designed with giftings, abilities and talents that were meant to be discovered, honed and shared.

Now is the time to move to a new level of understanding. Reach beyond your results to a place where you work in your Strengths everyday.

Although there are many resources to help you minimize your weaknesses, research shows that you can get a greater return from the same investment when you focus on improving your Strengths.

The focus of this workshop is to help you and your team to understand your Strengths, identify how they work in your life already, and create a plan to maximize those Strengths.

The following pages include numerous blank areas for a reason. They were meant to be used, both with introspective time and in group activities, to move your understanding of Strengths to a whole new level. With time and practice, you can develop your Strengths and dramatically improve your performance.

Even if you don't complete every aspect of this workbook during the workshop, please feel free to step into the other sections. Although not all of them are self-explanatory, there are several sections that you will be able to easily walk through and further develop an understanding and application of your Strengths.

In addition, there are numerous sections that require introspective time that is not easy to complete during a workshop or may be assigned as homework. You may only be able to start a section with just one of your Strengths before the group moves on to another section. To maximize your learning, complete the whole section in its entirety, working on your other Strengths as well.

This will help you extend your understanding and develop your ability to spend more time in your Strengths, letting the real you happily charge forward into a brighter tomorrow.

Figure out what you really love doing and use your strengths on a daily basis.

- Tom Rath

MY STRENGTHS REFERENCE

This section creates an easy to find overview of key elements about your Strengths. After you review all of the Strengths, complete the information about your top five Strengths by competing the My Top Strengths page.

STRENGTHS EXPLORATION | *Team Edition*

My Top Strengths

1

Strength:

Summary:

-
-
-

2

Strength:

Summary:

-
-
-

3

Strength:

Summary:

-
-
-

4

Strength:

Summary:

-
-
-

5

Strength:

Summary:

-
-
-

What lies behind us and what lies before us are tiny matters compared to what lies within us.

- Ralph Waldo Emerson

STRENGTHS REVIEW

There is more to understanding Strengths than just learning about your top few. What they are, how to leverage them and how to effectively work with others is equally important. As you learn about the Strengths system, this area provides unobstructed space to take notes and jot down observations that will deepen your understanding.

Notes:

Too many people overvalue what they are not and undervalue what they are.

- Malcom Forbes

STRENGTH DOMAINS

Natural inclinations cause us to want to group like things together. The more complex the concept, the stronger the desire to find similarities to categorize and simplify the understanding process.

There are several different ways to organize the full list of Strengths. The most common is to break them all down into four groups. Your instructor can review these categories of Strength Domains and, on a following page, help you complete the chart so you will have and easy way to categorize the Strengths.

Notes:

List the names of the domains in the top row. Then list each of the Strengths in the correct column.

Find your own 'sweet spot'. Take your talents and enjoy them, share them, expand them.

- Kofi Awoonor

INDIVIDUAL STRENGTHS

Knowing your Strengths is a great start, but when you can understand other's Strengths, you can become even more effective. By learning about each of the other Strengths, you will deepen your understanding of the value each can bring and have a better chance of helping others apply their Strengths in the right ways.

Unfortunately, we often place unfair expectations on others as we expect them to live up to our own level and abilities. Because our Strengths enable us to do certain things well, and often easily, we can discount the effort a particular task really takes. When others struggle with the same task, we attribute their failure to lack of effort or talent. In reality, they have different Strengths that set them up to excel in different areas. It is unfair to expect others to have your own Strengths. Understanding the other Strengths is the only way for you to begin to understand others potential correctly.

When you understand your team's differing Strengths, you deepen your understanding of how to best work and connect with them, creating a more enaging and effective team.

This next section allows you to take notes on each Strength to use as a future reference to maximize your team's abilities by understanding and helping them to correctly apply their Strengths.

Strength Name:

Domain: Example:

Team Members with this Strength:

Summary:

Strength Name:

Domain: Example:

Team Members with this Strength:

Summary:

Strength Name:

Domain: Example:

Team Members with this Strength:

Summary:

Strength Name:

Domain: Example:

Team Members with this Strength:

Summary:

Strength Name:

Domain: Example:

Team Members with this Strength:

Summary:

Strength Name:

Domain: Example:

Team Members with this Strength:

Summary:

Strength Name:

Domain: Example:

Team Members with this Strength:

Summary:

_____

Strength Name:

Domain: Example:

Team Members with this Strength:

Summary:

Strength Name:

Domain: Example:

Team Members with this Strength:

Summary:

Strength Name:

Domain: Example:

Team Members with this Strength:

Summary:

Strength Name:

Domain: Example:

Team Members with this Strength:

Summary:

Strength Name:

Domain: Example:

Team Members with this Strength:

Summary:

Strength Name:

Domain: Example:

Team Members with this Strength:

Summary:

Strength Name:

Domain: Example:

Team Members with this Strength:

Summary:

Strength Name:

Domain: Example:

Team Members with this Strength:

Summary:

Strength Name:

Domain: Example:

Team Members with this Strength:

Summary:

Strength Name:

Domain: Example:

Team Members with this Strength:

Summary:

Strength Name:

Domain: Example:

Team Members with this Strength:

Summary:

Strength Name:

Domain: Example:

Team Members with this Strength:

Summary:

Strength Name:

Domain: Example:

Team Members with this Strength:

Summary:

Strength Name:

Domain: Example:

Team Members with this Strength:

Summary:

Strength Name:

Domain: Example:

Team Members with this Strength:

Summary:

Strength Name:

Domain: Example:

Team Members with this Strength:

Summary:

Strength Name:

Domain: Example:

Team Members with this Strength:

Summary:

Strength Name:

Domain: Example:

Team Members with this Strength:

Summary:

Strength Name:

Domain: Example:

Team Members with this Strength:

Summary:

Strength Name:

Domain: Example:

Team Members with this Strength:

Summary:

Strength Name:

Domain: Example:

Team Members with this Strength:

Summary:

Strength Name:

Domain: Example:

Team Members with this Strength:

Summary:

Strength Name:

Domain: Example:

Team Members with this Strength:

Summary:

Strength Name:

Domain: Example:

Team Members with this Strength:

Summary:

_____

Strength Name:

Domain: Example:

Team Members with this Strength:

Summary:

Strength Name:

Domain: Example:

Team Members with this Strength:

Summary:

Strength Name:

Domain: Example:

Team Members with this Strength:

Summary:

Live in terms of your strong points. Magnify them. Let your weaknesses shirvel up and die from lack of nourishment.

- William Young Elliott

UNDERSTANDING YOUR TEAM'S STRENGTHS

Understanding your own strengths is valuable, but understanding the strengths of your team members is priceless.

Your objective is to work as a team to complete as much as you can in the allotted time on the following pages. List your strengths one at a time starting with Person A's first strength, then Person B's first strength and so on until you have listed through everyone's first strength. Then start on everyone's second strength.

Each person will describe their strength, the challenge of that strength, the benefit of that strength and the need they have to live out that Strength.

STRENGTHS EXPLORATION | *Team Edition*

Start with the top Strength for the first person. Then list that Strength, and describe the benefit that the Strength can bring when it is applied to what they do. Then move to the next column to the right on the facing page.

#	Strength	Team Member	Benefits I Bring w/ this Strength	

Continuing from the previous page, follow each row across to complete the final two boxes for that person and their Strength. Then move to the next person and complete the same process for everyone's top Strength before starting the process over with everyone's second Strength.

	Challenge this Strength Brings	What is Needed to Live Out this Strength

STRENGTHS EXPLORATION | *Team Edition*

Start with the top Strength for the first person. Then list that Strength, and describe the benefit that the Strength can bring when it is applied to what they do. Then move to the next column to the right on the facing page.

#	Strength	Team Member	Benefits I Bring w/ this Strength	

Continuing from the previous page, follow each row across to complete the final two boxes for that person and their Strength. Then move to the next person and complete the same process for everyone's top Strength before starting the process over with everyone's second Strength.

	Challenge this Strength Brings	What is Needed to Live Out this Strength

Start with the top Strength for the first person. Then list that Strength, and describe the benefit that the Strength can bring when it is applied to what they do. Then move to the next column to the right on the facing page.

#	Strength	Team Member	Benefits I Bring w/ this Strength	

Continuing from the previous page, follow each row across to complete the final two boxes for that person and their Strength. Then move to the next person and complete the same process for everyone's top Strength before starting the process over with everyone's second Strength.

	Challenge this Strength Brings	What is Needed to Live Out this Strength

STRENGTHS EXPLORATION | *Team Edition*

Start with the top Strength for the first person. Then list that Strength, and describe the benefit that the Strength can bring when it is applied to what they do. Then move to the next column to the right on the facing page.

#	Strength	Team Member	Benefits I Bring w/ this Strength	

Continuing from the previous page, follow each row across to complete the final two boxes for that person and their Strength. Then move to the next person and complete the same process for everyone's top Strength before starting the process over with everyone's second Strength.

	Challenge this Strength Brings	What is Needed to Live Out this Strength

I can do things you cannot, you can do things I cannot; together we can do great things.

- *Mother Theresa*

Understanding the Strengths of your team helps you to understand who has similar Strengths and who has different Strengths. Knowing similarities allows teams to group Strengths together to maximize the positive change they want to create. Knowing the differences allows teams to lean on each others Strengths to fill in gaps and help support one another. The Team Grid also provides an easy way to look up everyone's Strengths as well as allowing teams to identify Strengths that are not represented on the team.

STRENGTHS EXPLORATION | *Team Edition*

In the very top row, write in the names of either the categories, themes or domains of Strengths given by the instructor. Simply use only the first column if not using domain categories. Start by listing your Strenghts, then complete the rest of the grid with everyone's Strengths.

Team Name	#				
	1				
	2				
	3				
	4				
	5				
	1				
	2				
	3				
	4				
	5				
	1				
	2				
	3				
	4				
	5				
	1				
	2				
	3				
	4				
	5				
	1				
	2				
	3				
	4				
	5				
	1				
	2				
	3				
	4				
	5				
	1				
	2				
	3				
	4				
	5				

In the very top row, write in the names of either the categories, themes or domains of Strengths given by the instructor. Simply use only the first column if not using domain categories. Start by listing your Strenghts, then complete the rest of the grid with everyone's Strengths.

Team Name	#				
	1				
	2				
	3				
	4				
	5				
	1				
	2				
	3				
	4				
	5				
	1				
	2				
	3				
	4				
	5				
	1				
	2				
	3				
	4				
	5				
	1				
	2				
	3				
	4				
	5				
	1				
	2				
	3				
	4				
	5				
	1				
	2				
	3				
	4				
	5				

STRENGTHS EXPLORATION | *Team Edition*

In the very top row, write in the names of either the categories, themes or domains of Strengths given by the instructor. Simply use only the first column if not using domain categories. Start by listing your Strenghts, then complete the rest of the grid with everyone's Strengths.

Team Name	#				
	1				
	2				
	3				
	4				
	5				
	1				
	2				
	3				
	4				
	5				
	1				
	2				
	3				
	4				
	5				
	1				
	2				
	3				
	4				
	5				
	1				
	2				
	3				
	4				
	5				
	1				
	2				
	3				
	4				
	5				
	1				
	2				
	3				
	4				
	5				

Team Grid w/o Domains: Write in your name and Strengths, then list the names of everyone else on your team, then write in their Strengths.

Names	Strength 1	Strength 2	Strength 3	Strength 4	Strength 5

You can run a business any way you like, but you'll run it better if you build it around your strengths.

- *Duncan Bannatyne*

OPTIMUM VS. OVERUSED

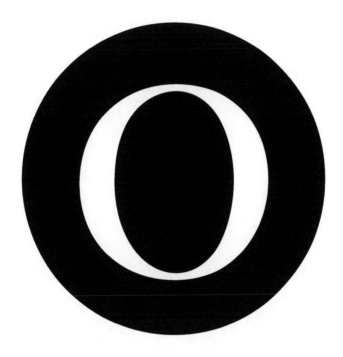

Just as too much of a good thing can be bad for you, so can displaying too much of your Strengths create a shortcoming.

Overusing your Strengths keeps others from experiencing your Strengths at their best. When overused, Strengths become weapons that depreciate relational capital and diminish teamwork. Other titles given when Strengths are overused are Overplayed, Shadow Side, and Basement, along with a few others. In this workbook we will use the term Overused to describe when a Strength is overextended, where continued application no longer adds value to the situation as a whole.

Take a moment and think about how your Strengths may have been overused in the past. What happened to the task? What happened to the relationships?

Take a few moments and describe 2 or 3 occasions when one or more of your Strengths were overused. Include what happened to the task or the relationships around each occasion.

Examples of Strengths Overused:

1.

2.

3.

Write in a brief description that describes what happens when your Strengths are at their Optimum and again when they are Overused. This can serve as a reference point for understanding why things are not going the way you would like and help to bring you back on track to the optimum levels.

Strength	Optimum	Overused
1.		
2.		
3.		
4.		
5.		

Accept yourself, your strengths, your weaknesses, your truths, and know what tools you have to fulfill your purpose.

- *Steve Maraboli*

TRIGGER STRENGTH

One of your top Strengths acts differently than all the others. When this special *Trigger* Strength connects with something, it activates and engages you in the process. It is intertwined with all of the other Strengths because when this Trigger Strength is pulled on, you and your Strengths are then energized to move forward.

When you understand which one it is, you can take advantage of it by intentionally using it to trigger yourself to get things done!

Write out your top Strengths below and complete the checkboxes to help identify your Trigger Strength.

		I use this Strength nearly every day.	I can recall using this Strength as much or more than the others.	This Strength drives me.	If all other Strengths are absent, I still move forward.	I get more done when I lead with this Strength	TOTALS
1							
2							
3							
4							
5							

The Strength with the most checkmarks is your Trigger Strength.

If several have the same count, take a moment to think about each Strength, one at a time, to consider which one is the most powerful trigger, that when pulled, engages you to act. Write that Trigger Strength in the trigger spot that touches all of the other Strengths, then write in all of your Strengths in order around the Trigger Strength.

This provides a visual reminder of your Trigger Strength.

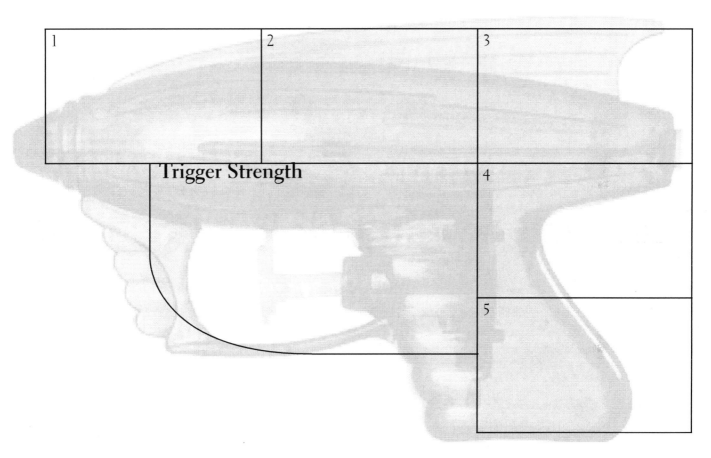

1. What happens when your Trigger Strength is activated?

2. How can you leverage your Trigger Strength to help you complete projects you feel stuck on?

He who knows others is wise; He who knows himself is enlightened.

- Lao-tzu

% I WORK IN MY STRENGTHS

One of the objectives of this Workbook is to help you move into your Strengths more. Working in them 70% - 90% of the week energizes you to do your best each and every day. Everyone understands that there are always a few tasks that drain you but are a necessary part of your role's responsibilities. But, when those draining activities are minimized and the time spent working in your Strengths is maximized, it results in a happier, healthier and more productive you.

The first step in this change process is to identify the starting point. Where are you right now? How much time is spent working in your Strengths? With what you understand about your Strengths, chart out on the graphs between 0% to 100% of the amount of time you feel you are working in areas where you get to work in your Strengths.

Identifying how your time is spent is the first part of the process to move you into working in your Strengths more of the time. In general, activities can be divided into three categories; Draining, Neutral and Energizing. Take a moment below to think about how you spend your time and which tasks fit in which category.

Categories:

- Draining: Tasks that pull energy away from other areas and you would much rather avoid if possible.

- Neutral: Tasks that don't thrill you but they also don't excite you. They are just things that need to be done and so you do them.

- Energizing: Tasks that you look forward to energize and excite you. These are the things that you often get 'lost' in the middle of, forgetting everything else.

Examples of tasks that are Draining:

Examples of tasks that are Neutral:

Examples of tasks that are Energizing:

Now that you have an idea of which tasks fit in each category, it is time to chart out the amount of time spent in each category.

Use your best guess as to what percentage of your time in an average week is currently spent in each category. Your percentage across these three categories should add up to 100%.

This is your starting point for creating a frame of reference for the improvement that is coming. The goal is to spend more and more time with Energizing tasks. These are the areas where you come alive and your Strengths are best used.

Complete the graph below by filling in the percentage of each week that you spend in each category, creating a bar graph that starts at 0% and fills across. All three should add up to a total of 100%.

Example: Draining = 30%   Neutral = 50%   Energizing = 20%

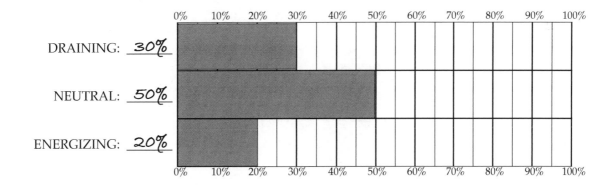

Percent I work in my Strengths Reference Point

Today's Date: _____

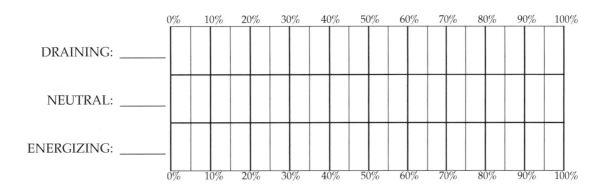

To identify the progress you make working more in your Strengths, use this form every quarter to re-chart your results. The Strengths Tracking pages will help you identify the specific tasks and clarify the percentages.

After completing the tracking forms for a week, chart in the percentages below to identify your progress.

Date Completed: _____

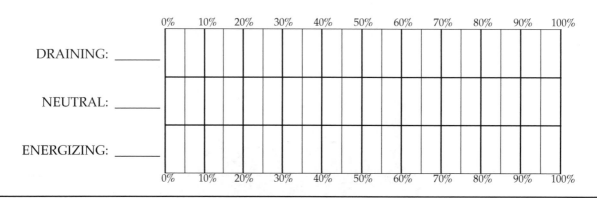

Date Completed: _____

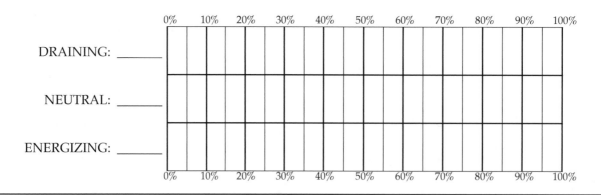

Date Completed: _____

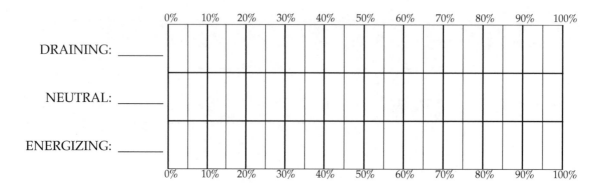

Date Completed: _____

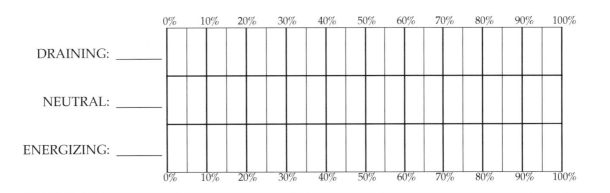

Date Completed: _____

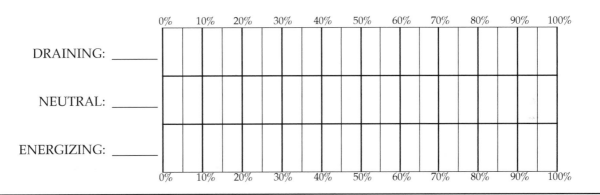

Date Completed: _____

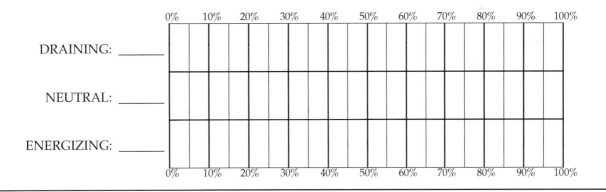

Date Completed: _____

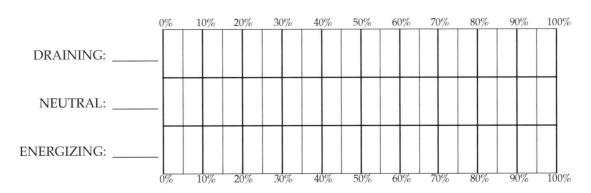

Choose the path to an authentic, passionate life by choosing to focus most of your energy on strengthening your strengths.

- Barrie Davenport

STRENGTH TRACKING

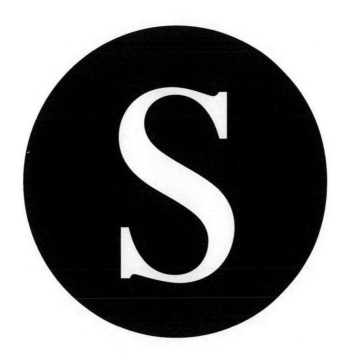

Tracking how your work time is spent will help you to see the progress you are making to work in the area of your Strengths more. Select an average week to track the tasks you do indicating if the tasks are a Drainer, Neutral or Energizer. Briefly describe the task then write in an amount of time you spend doing it. It may be helpful to group similar tasks together.

To ease in the calculation process, consider keeping the time increments in fractions of an hour, i.e. .15, .25, .5, etc.

Tracking Dates: _____

Draining	Neutral	Energizing	Describe the Task	Amount of Time Spent
X			Completing online forms to request information to complete the Harrison Project	.25

Tracking Dates: _____

Draining	Neutral	Energizing	Describe the Task	Amount of Time Spent

Tracking Dates: _____

Draining	Neutral	Energizing	Describe the Task	Amount of Time Spent

Tracking Dates: _____

Draining	Neutral	Energizing	Describe the Task	Amount of Time Spent

Tracking Dates: _____

Draining	Neutral	Energizing	Describe the Task	Amount of Time Spent

Tracking Dates: _____

Draining	Neutral	Energizing	Describe the Task	Amount of Time Spent

Tracking Dates: _____

Draining	Neutral	Energizing	Describe the Task	Amount of Time Spent

Tracking Dates: _____

Draining	Neutral	Energizing	Describe the Task	Amount of Time Spent

Tracking Dates: _____

Draining	Neutral	Energizing	Describe the Task	Amount of Time Spent

Tracking Dates: _____

Draining	Neutral	Energizing	Describe the Task	Amount of Time Spent

Tracking Dates: _____

Draining	Neutral	Energizing	Describe the Task	Amount of Time Spent

Tracking Dates: _____

Draining	Neutral	Energizing	Describe the Task	Amount of Time Spent

Now that you've completed a week's worth of tracking on the previous pages, it is time to summarize and add up the hours to find your actual results.

1.   Summarize by listing the top three types of tasks in each category that used the greatest amount of time.

DRAINING Tasks: NEUTRAL Tasks: ENERGIZING Tasks:

-                                  -   -

-                                  -   -

-                                  -   -

2.   Then add up the amount of time spent in each category from all tasks on your tracking sheets.

Total DRAINING Time: Total NEUTRAL Time: Total ENERGIZING Time:

_____   _____   _____

3.   Finally, add up the total of all tracked hours.

        GRAND TOTAL OF ALL TRACKED HOURS: _____

4.   Complete the calculation below by writing in the total time spent in that category by the total number of all hours you tracked. Then multiply that number by 100 to find the percentage of time you spend in a week in that category. Repeat for each of the three categories and use this information on the next page.

i.e. <u>16</u> Draining hours ÷ <u>40</u> Grand Total hours = .4   Then multiply .4 by 100 = 40%

	DRAINING	**NEUTRAL**	**ENERGIZING**
Time Spent:			
(Divide)	÷	÷	÷
Grand Total of ALL Tracked Hours:			
(Multiply)	X	X	X
	100	100	100
Percentage:	%	%	%

5.   Chart in your results in the previous chapter, % I Work in My Strengths, and compare to your intial estimation and subsequent results.

Repeat the process as often as you would like.

Tracking Dates: _____

	DRAINING	**NEUTRAL**	**ENERGIZING**
Time Spent:			
(Divide)	÷	÷	÷
Grand Total of ALL Tracked Hours:			
(Multiply)	X	X	X
	100	100	100
Percentage:	%	%	%

STRENGTHS EXPLORATION | *Team Edition*

Tracking Dates: _____

	DRAINING	NEUTRAL	ENERGIZING
Time Spent:			
(Divide)	÷	÷	÷
Grand Total of ALL Tracked Hours:			
(Multiply)	X	X	X
	100	100	100
Percentage:	%	%	%

Tracking Dates: _____

	DRAINING	NEUTRAL	ENERGIZING
Time Spent:			
(Divide)	÷	÷	÷
Grand Total of ALL Tracked Hours:			
(Multiply)	X	X	X
	100	100	100
Percentage:	%	%	%

Tracking Dates: _____

	DRAINING	NEUTRAL	ENERGIZING
Time Spent:			
(Divide)	÷	÷	÷
Grand Total of ALL Tracked Hours:			
(Multiply)	X	X	X
	100	100	100
Percentage:	%	%	%

Tracking Dates: _____

	DRAINING	**NEUTRAL**	**ENERGIZING**
Time Spent:			
(Divide)	÷	÷	÷
Grand Total of ALL Tracked Hours:			
(Multiply)	X	X	X
	100	100	100
Percentage:	%	%	%

Tracking Dates: _____

	DRAINING	**NEUTRAL**	**ENERGIZING**
Time Spent:			
(Divide)	÷	÷	÷
Grand Total of ALL Tracked Hours:			
(Multiply)	X	X	X
	100	100	100
Percentage:	%	%	%

Tracking Dates: _____

	DRAINING	**NEUTRAL**	**ENERGIZING**
Time Spent:			
(Divide)	÷	÷	÷
Grand Total of ALL Tracked Hours:			
(Multiply)	X	X	X
	100	100	100
Percentage:	%	%	%

The person born with a talent they were meant to use will find their greatest happiness in using it.

- Johann Wolfgang von Goethe

JOB RESPONSIBILITIES

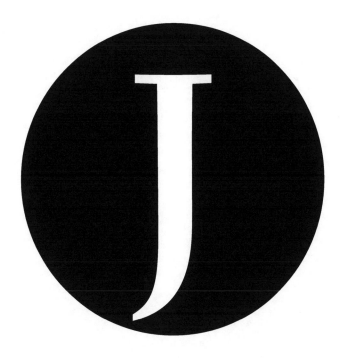

Taking your Strength training to the next level includes leveraging your Strengths to do a better job completing your top responsibilities. On the following page, you will identify your top job responsibilities and then give careful consideration toward which Strengths apply and can be used to increase the quality of your work — while becoming more engaged. Some connections are easier to make than others, but with a little creative thinking from an outside perspective (and possibly some help from a team member) you'll be able to see how to apply your Strengths and accomplish more, feeling better and more alive.

Brief description of a top job responsibility.

How you can focus on applying one or more of your Strengths to accel in this area.

A

-

-

-

-

B

-

-

-

-

C

-

-

-

-

D

-

-

-

-

Without continual growth and progress such words as improvement, achievement and success have no meaning.

- Benjamin Franklin

CONTINUING THE CHANGE

In order to continue to develop your Strengths it takes a combination of external and internal motivators. Continuing to discuss your Strengths with your team is essential. Complimenting each other when Strengths bring value to the project and the team helps encouarge more of the same. In addition, it helps to also create a personal plan to continue the change on your own.

A little bit of planning now can make a huge difference in how well you develop and expand your Strengths.

On a scale of 1-10, how important is it to you to continue to develop your Strengths?

If you indicated 7 or above, congratulations! You are ready to take the next step. Here are a few recommendations:

1. **Today**, set a date to start the Strength Tracking Form

2. **Weekly**, review your Quick Reference sheet

3. **Monthly**, review your My Strengths Reference section with a coworker or the entire team

4. **Quarterly**, complete the Strengths Tracking sheets and reassess the time spent in each Strength working toward 70-90%

What else could you do to continue to develop your Strengths?

What steps do you want to take to continue to develop your Strengths?

How likely is it that you will follow through each of the steps you indicated you wanted to take?

How can you include accountability to help you continue with these steps?

Just do what you do best.

- Red Auerbach

QUICK REFERENCE

It isn't easy to keep new information at the forefront of your mind. However, if you want to reap the long-term benefits of leveraging your strengths, you need a way to remember what you are now learning. The Quick Reference is a tool that can help. Complete and post this half sheet somewhere where you will see it every day. It will be a reminder to think about your Strengths and how to use them throughout the day.

Posting a copy at work on your wall or door can be a reminder for both you and those you work with. This is especially valuable when you and your team members commit to help each other to continually bring improvement.

So, complete, post and keep focused on your Strengths!

My Top Strengths

_____
Name

Top Strengths

-

-

-

-

-

My Top Strengths

_____
Name

Top Strengths

-

-

-

-

-

My Top Strengths

Name

Top Strengths

-

-

-

-

-

My Top Strengths

Name

Top Strengths

-

-

-

-

-

Exercise A

Exercise B

Exercise B

Exercise C

Exercise C

Made in the USA
Columbia, SC
05 October 2017